BOUNTY–
the tale of a dog

Patricia M Wilnecker

By the same author:
non-fiction

High Street Murders 1598
Published by Poole Museum Services

A History of Upper Parkstone (beginning to 1939)
Upper Parkstone in the Second World War
More Recollections of Old Upper Parkstone
Published by Patricia M Wilnecker

fiction:
The Bountifull Gyfte
Published by Patricia M Wilnecker

Published by Patricia M Wilnecker
73 Gwynne Road
Parkstone
Poole, Dorset
BH12 2AR

First published 1992

copyright P M Wilnecker

British Library Cataloguing in Publication Data.
A catalogue record for this book is available from the British Library.

All rights reserved

Typeset and printed in Great Britain by
Bourne Press Limited, Bournemouth

ISBN 0 9513971 4 1

For my sister Vi Maitland

CONTENTS

Page

CHAPTER 1.	WE MEET	1
CHAPTER 2.	EARLY DAYS	7
CHAPTER 3.	THE HUNTER	10
CHAPTER 4.	PROBLEMS	14
CHAPTER 5.	TRAINING	18
CHAPTER 6.	FAVOURITE WALKS	21
CHAPTER 7.	SUMMER HOLIDAYS	27
CHAPTER 8.	BOUNTY GETS LOST	31
CHAPTER 9.	THE OPERATION	33
CHAPTER 10.	BOUNTY'S FRIENDS	36
CHAPTER 11.	NARROW ESCAPES	40
CHAPTER 12.	ENCOUNTERS WITH OTHER ANIMALS	44
CHAPTER 13.	THE FIRST AND LAST DOG SHOW	47
CHAPTER 14.	THE STOLEN CAR	50
CHAPTER 15.	WORRYING TIMES	52
CHAPTER 16.	BOUNTY'S FIRST BIRTHDAY	55

Chapter 1
We Meet

I felt desperately lonely that October night, leaves fluttering against the rain-dashed window pane, sitting my myself, listening to the tick of the clock. Suddenly I couldn't stand it any longer and with a wail of despair, flung myself on the settee and had a good, healthy weep.

Don't misunderstand me, I have very good friends and relations but that night with the depressing thought of winter just around the corner, somehow I felt in a vacuum ... little did I know what fate had in store as not ten miles away, in kennels, an event had happened that very day which was to change my entire life!

Those well-meaning friends, knowing I took solitary walks and worrying about my safety, often hinted I should have a dog for company and protection but I made the usual excuses - they were a tie - I liked walking the Dorset Coastal Path which would be too dangerous with the crumbling cliffs - a dog would spoil the garden (I HAD been a keen gardener!) and so on...

I think it was at Old Sarum, that spectacular windswept earthwork overlooking the city of Salisbury that I began considering the idea seriously. It was a cold day I remember, so my friends and I were picnicking in the car and watching people walking their dogs while we played a kind of game, choosing the breed of dog WE would like.

Now my brother-in-law Jim is a farmer, and he and my sister Vi have a Border Collie called Sharp that always gives me a great welcome, looking at me with worshipful brown eyes, resting his warm chin on my lap and leaning lovingly against my legs. In my ignorance I imagined all dogs came like that! Well, the germ of an idea took root in my mind and at odd moments I thought seriously about getting a puppy. I could cope - of COURSE I could! We had one when I was a child, Rex, a Welsh Collie but I conveniently forgot that mother had all the responsibilities of training and walks, so really my knowledge was pretty limited.

Chatting over the hedge one day with Peg, my neighbour I mentioned I was toying with the idea of getting a puppy. I had an escape-proof back garden with plenty of grass, a couple of ponds with frogs, and some flower beds and borders. The ponds were netted to keep magpies from stealing the frogs, as I had opened my back door one day and startled a black and white villain which flew away, dropping something from its beak. An amazed frog landed by the pond and staggered back with all its arms and legs intact - saved in the nick of time! So, the ponds were covered in netting which should also keep out a puppy.

"They had a lovely Jack Russell cross at the pet shop," Peg told me encouragingly.

Warming to the idea I said, "Jack Russell, now THAT'S a thought!" assuming it would behave like a scaled down version of Sharp while taking up less room. I had never even spoken to a Jack Russell or its owner and knew even less about the breed's temperament. Nevertheless, without further ado I paid a visit to the pet shop which is about a quarter of a mile away, but as luck would have it the puppy had been sold and they had no others of any type or breed in stock.

Now once I have made up my mind to do something, NOTHING will stop me so I went home and searched through Yellow Pages. Another pet shop owner said "We've a German Shepherd/Dobermann cross coming in at the weekend."

"Er - no thanks!" I said quickly as I didn't think I could cope with anything that size or temperament and rang the R.S.P.C.A. Shelter at Ringwood. It must have been fate, because three times I tried and the line was engaged, so I resorted to Yellow Pages again, this time phoning kennels not far from my sister's farm.

"Yes, we've plenty of puppies," the owner told me.

"What breed?" I asked hopefully.

"All pedigree Jack Russell's" he replied. Fate had taken a hand again and I knew I was committed.

"I'll be with you in half an hour," I said, putting a cardboard box with soft cloths in it next to me in the car for my expected new arrival and heading for the kennels.

The owner met me at the gate and gave me a guided tour. There were tiny pups, squealing and squirming, and larger ones bouncing and wagging for attention but even to my inexperienced eye they all looked far too young to leave their mothers.

"Have you any that I could take home today?" I asked hopefully and he led me to some pens in a field by a wood.

"These are ready. The pups are just six weeks old," he said, indicating a rough haired bitch called Solo and her offspring. "I'll leave you to get acquainted." Suiting action to words, he walked away and started chatting to a nearby tractor driver, leaving me alone with the animals. Solo had four pups. One was £100 he told me and the rest £80. They were known as 'Parson Jack Russell's', the original type with long legs, not the squat, short-legged variety.

This must be one of the hardest decisions I shall ever have to make, I thought to myself, and whispered to the pups, "Which one of you is going to share my life, then?" They all looked as adorable as each other. Solo gazed at me with anxious brown eyes, having been through this before. I tried to think of all the things you should look for when buying a pup but 'don't be tempted to take the quietest or the weakest' was the only point I could remember. Then one little fellow, white with chestnut brown ears and eye patches and a wide white 'road' down his forehead broke away from the rest and started chasing a leaf. "You look playful, will you be my little chum?" I asked, picking him up carefully. He was soft and warm, snuggling contentedly against my jacket, no bigger than my hand. "Made your mind up?" called the kennel owner. "I THINK so," I answered hesitantly, hoping I had made the right decision but afraid to commit myself.

"Oh, you've a little beauty there, he's the pick of the bunch! That one's £100."

I thought smugly I obviously had a talent for spotting a good dog, and walked away from Solo without turning around, unable to look her in the eye, hoping she was busy with her family while I carried off her best son.

"What will you call him?" asked the kennel owner as I gently placed the pup in my cardboard box.

My historical novel, "The Bountifull Gyfte" had just gone to print so without hesitation I answered, "Bounty."

"That's a good name," he said "We haven't had one of those. I'll enter it on his pedigree."

"He will have lovely walks," I assured Bounty's ex-owner. "I often go to Purbeck." This is an area of windswept chalk and limestone hills, culminating in the chalk stacks of Old Harry Rocks in the east, bordered on one side by the English Channel and on the other by Poole Harbour. Part of it is owned by the National Trust and is scheduled as an area of outstanding natural beauty.

"You'll have to watch it there," he said warningly. "He'll go down badger and fox holes - you can't stop him, it's instinctive. Both Solo and your pup's sire, Butcher are working Jack Russells and go out with the hunt every winter. Do you know it's illegal to dig dogs out of badger and fox holes?"

I felt a warning, apprehensive tingle run up my spine. Had I done the right thing? The only animals Sharp ran after were cows in the course of his farm duties! Still, I repressed my fears and at least had the sense to check on Bounty's dietary requirements and inoculations before setting off with him in his cardboard box, kept firmly in its place by the car seatbelt. I felt every bit as proud as a mother bringing her firstborn home from the maternity hospital. I had never been in that position myself. As youngest of three I stayed at home with mother until she died at the age of eighty-nine, father having died when I was four years old. This meant Bounty was the first living creature for which I was to have complete responsibility and which depended on me for everything.

Vi's farm was nearby. I hadn't told anyone except my neighbour Peg that I was getting a dog so I thought I would give her a surprise. Bounty snuggled down in his box, not minding the car at all and after a few minutes drive we rolled up at the farmhouse door.

"Hello," said Vi with a grin, sticking her head out, "and to what do we owe this pleasure?"

"Come and see what I've got!" I said mysteriously.

She came over to the car and peeped in at the window. "Oh - you've bought a GUINEA PIG!" she cried.

"It's a PUPPY!" I retorted indignantly, mother tiger defending her young. "A little Jack Russell and he's just six weeks old. Keep Sharp away, he mustn't mix with other dogs until he's had his full set of injections at thirteen weeks.

"Oh, you dear little soul!" she purred, lifting him with one hand and giving him a cuddle while he gazed up at her short-sightedly, licking her face.

"Well, I mustn't stop," I said importantly, "This was only a flying visit - I've a 'child' to feed!" and off we drove very carefully so I wouldn't disturb him, and on arrival carried his box into my kitchen which fortunately has a vinyl floor covering. This was to be his new home. After spreading newspapers around I produced a dish for his natural yoghurt or raw mince, depending on the time of day, and another for his water. He ate a hearty meal then went out to explore the escape-proof back garden. He was so tiny, he couldn't negotiate the steps up to my back door so I placed a brick on each tread to make it easier for him, and he quickly learned to use them.

Full of good intentions, I was determined that he would never share my bedroom (ho-ho-ho!) so was prepared to be 'cruel to be kind' and ignore any whimpers in the night. Bounty also gave me the first insight into his strong character by NOT whimpering and settled in beautifully. (I hardly slept a wink.)

Next day, Joan and I had planned to go walking. We had been friends since our schooldays and when I wasn't going on solitary expeditions we walked together. She and her husband John always owned dogs, but after the death of Jamie their West Highland terrier a couple of years before, they hadn't acquired another one.

Confidingly, I told her on the telephone that I had something to show her. Arriving at her house I popped Bounty into the pocket of my Barbour jacket and walked in, a smug smile on my face. His little head peeped out as Joan came to the door.

"Aah!" she murmured, enraptured, making a great fuss of him, "So you've got a dog at last!"

Even at that early age he was inquisitive and gave her bungalow a thorough tour of inspection, sniffing each room.

We decided it would be all right to go for our walk as long as we kept well away from other dogs. I had brought a bag with me to carry him in so we headed for the Purbeck hills in the car, Joan cuddling Bounty on her lap on an old towel in case of 'accidents'. The kennel man had explained that the pups were 'hardened off' by living in their outdoor runs and wouldn't be affected by the cold, so we drove along a picturesque lane that wound through the hills to the tiny thatched village of Kimmeridge with its remote, cliff-ringed bay. Although it was November the sun glinted invitingly on the calm sea as we climbed carefully with our 'precious burden' to the water's edge. Bounty had to leave the bag for his calls of nature so I placed him between the rocks on a patch of sand which was washed clean by the waves. It was bare of any human or animal footprints so quite hygienic for Bounty. He squatted dutifully, leaving less mess than a seagull and we popped him back into the bag, carrying him along paths that were deserted at that time of year. The little fellow was very good, peeping out short-sightedly at all the new sights and sounds, interested in everything.

So there we were - the very inexperienced new owner and my trusting little dependent, I still not realising how much my life was to change - waiting for the future to unfold...

Chapter 2
Early Days

Christmas was almost upon us and Bounty took up more time that I thought possible. Fortunately, and unusually for me I had bought most of my presents early that year so at least THEY were no problem. No so Bounty! Being virtually confined to the house and garden, he wanted to play ALL the time! I thought he would have slept more but he seemed tireless. Every evening at around 6.45pm he had a 'funny five minutes', racing around the sitting room, behind the arm chairs and settee like an express train, full of exuberance. His little teeth were like needles - luckily not very destructive to the furniture with the exception of a spectacular display with a raffia waste paper basket, discovering he could unravel the carpet and every day causing the bathroom rug to arrive mysteriously in the hall - oh no, he preferred ankles and hands! I decided after receiving many scratches and scars that an anti-tetanus injection would be a good thing, so set about organising one.

I thought his behaviour would improve as the days went by, but I never seemed to have any peace. Joan was very good, inviting me for meals and 'puppy sitting' for a while to let me relax, otherwise I'd have gone potty! I even entertained fleeting, half-formed ideas of enquiring to see if the kennels would take him back, he was so unruly, disobedient and apparently unloving. Where was the 'quick to learn, affectionate little dog' the kennel man had described? (I realise now I was expecting far too much, too soon. The poor little soul was only ten weeks old!) I knew deep down though I would never admit defeat, and however troublesome he was I couldn't return him. My bed was made, and I would lie on it.

There WERE good times of course - a lick from a tiny pink tongue, a gaze from limpid hazel eyes, but was that only cupboard love, I asked myself?

Well, as I said, Christmas was upon us and Joan invited us to her party along with some friends of hers I knew slightly.

"Are you SURE you want Bounty?" I asked.

"Of course!" she said. She is a dog-aholic, and Bounty can do no wrong in her eyes.

We must have looked funny at the party. I brought a selection of cardboard boxes with me - not as a party game - for the ladies to put their feet in and so save ankles and tights from little teeth! Joan took photos, I remember. Bounty thought the party was great. He loves company and looking back I suppose he must have been bored at home with just me, a fifty-six year old to play with.

For the Christmas holidays we were invited to the farm. Sharp was up to date with his inoculations so the vet said that would be all right, to my relief.

Tradition in our family was to go to the Christmas Eve midnight service in the lovely old village church at Lytchett Matravers. I put Bounty upstairs in his cardboard box along with his 'brother' - a stuffed toy dog he always slept with, which he'd had since I'd owned him. He was quite used to being left at home while I shot out to buy food, but the farm was a strange place and NO WAY was he going to be left alone. (We didn't like to leave him in the same room as Sharp, who was naturally rather possessive about his own territory.) You wouldn't think such a little pup could emit such loud, soulful howls and yaps!

"I'd better not leave him," I said, feeling sorry for the poor little fellow. He must have thought he was being abandoned. "You go on," so they did, leaving us watching TV alone in the farmhouse.

Now there is an old Dorset tradition set to verse by Thomas Hardy that says at midnight on Christmas Eve the oxen kneel to commemorate the birth of Christ in a stable. Being Dorset born, I'd always wondered about this and thought here was my chance to see if it were true. At ten minutes to midnight I lifted Bounty into my arms and went out into the crisp, still, frosty night air. His little body was soft and warm and I held him close. In the distance a vixen gave her yelping cry and the evening star hung low over the village beyond the dark woods. I crept softly to the cowshed and peeped in. The animals, sensing my presence, stirred. Checking my watch, I saw there were still five minutes to go - when a peculiar feeling came over me - I was an interloper, I had no business being there, it was no place for humans at this moment in time, so turning away I took Bounty back to the warmth of the farmhouse ... It was very strange, and even more odd as I have since read of two other separate incidents where people had similar experiences. Now I shall probably never know for sure if the oxen kneel, but then again, I won't know if they DON'T, so that will keep the mystery alive.

Chapter 3

The Hunter

I was determined that Bounty would be a well-behaved, biddable dog. Having heard the saying, "There is no such thing as a bad dog, only a bad owner," I realised the shaping of his character was up to me.

With this responsibility in mind I regarded my very comfortable three piece suite, as soft as a duvet with a cream background and decorated with pink and beige roses - NOT ideal when you have a dog! Bounty decided it was to HIS taste, too.

"DOWN" I commanded firmly, lifting him off, but back he jumped immediately. Over and over I repeated the performance and equally determinedly so did he! He really was a dominant little fellow in those days.

I poured out my troubles to Joan. She was no help!

"Well, you must remember, it is HIS home too," she told me.

"Yes, of course, but..."

He still sits on the suite. At least the covers can be removed and washed - but oh, the battles to stuff them again - I have to ask Peg to help me! I had my revenge on Joan though. Her daughter Jill had been staying with her and slept on a 'Put-U-Up' bed on the floor. We were visiting and Bounty had the run of the house as usual (remember, he could do no wrong in Joan's eyes).

It had been quiet for a while. "Where's Bounty?" I asked apprehensively. We called, but he ignored us as per normal so we began to search the house.

Jill suddenly gave an exasperated yell. "BOUNTY — you little SO-AND-SO! Look what he's done!" And there, in the middle of her bed for all to see he had deposited his 'biggies'! That, however was his final fling. Afterwards he was completely housetrained and never did anything like it again, so at least, slowly, we were achieving something.

He always went to bed in the kitchen with his toys - the favourite being his aforementioned 'brother', the soft toy dog which was bigger than he was when I got him. He would worry it like a rat and play with it for hours, finally snuggling up to it at bedtime.

If he had been REALLY exasperating I would send him into the kitchen with a very cross voice and without his toys. This had only happened twice as I felt a complete heel and let him out after five minutes, but it must have had a lasting effect because I only had to say threateningly, "Do you want to go in the kitchen?" and he would stop being naughty. This was indeed a breakthrough!

Eventually, after what seemed a lifetime his thirteen weeks 'quarantine' was up. I took him to the Vet for his final injection and he didn't bat an eyelid. At last we could venture out into the wide world without fear of meeting germ-ridden animals! I had marked the calendar, 'Bounty's Release!' but felt it was MINE, too.

We called for Joan of course and drove to Worth Matravers, a lovely village of old stone houses clustered around a duck pond, where we left the car and walked the winding path to the sea at Winspit. Bounty was interested in everything - there were such exciting smells everywhere, his little nose could hardly sniff fast enough. In fact, his first experience with water was the Worth Matravers village pond. There swam ducks, and the pond's margins were liberally covered with solid looking green duckweed. Already the Jack Russell character was developing and he spotted the ducks, giving chase with great glee only to find the duckweed wasn't solid at all and melted beneath his paws! "HELP!" his eyes seemed to say as he submerged. Luckily he was still on the lead and I hauled him out. He bobbed up, looking very surprised but completely undismayed and stood grinning while we removed duckweed from his head and back, drying him off with our handkerchiefs.

After the pond incident, we went to the Scott Arms at Kingston for lunch. It stands in a beautiful situation on the top of the range of hills overlooking Corfe Castle. AND they admit well-behaved dogs! Praying that ours would be, Joan and I went in and ordered a couple of 'Ploughman's Lunches', crisp brown bread, a lump of cheese, tomato, lettuce, cucumber, pickle and an apple - delicious! It was quite busy that day and three ladies asked if they could share our table. One was obviously an American and staying with the others on holiday. We were soon happily chatting together and discovered they didn't know Purbeck very well, so we recommended places for them to visit. Then Bounty made his appearance from under the table where he had been sitting quietly, being a 'well-behaved dog'.

"Oh, what an ADORABLE little puppy!" they cooed. Bounty sat, switching to his 'adorable' expression. "What do you call him?"

"Bounty," I told them.

"What an unusual name, where did it come from?" asked one.

Joan chipped in, "My friend is an author - she's just written an historical novel called 'The Bountifull Gyfte' set in this area and he is named after it."

I nudged her beneath the table, embarrassed.

"You're an author? How wonderful! May we take your photo?" they asked, and we all dutifully posed together with Bounty in the foreground.

"We MUST buy your book!" they said reverently. (That always makes me chuckle. I'm only ME!)

"The National Trust Shop in Corfe Castle!" Joan impressed on them as they waved their goodbyes and drove off, poste haste to buy copies.

★ ★ ★

Another day, Vi and I took him to Lymington and walked on the saltmarshes overlooking the Isle of Wight. He was about six months old by then and we let him run free as usual.

"Oh, look!" I called, "a baby rabbit." It seemed to be hurt, as it walked rather lolloped but didn't have the dreadful swollen eyes of myxomatosis. The trouble was, Bounty saw it too and was after it like a shot! With a pounce, he caught it, worrying it like an old slipper and at once the little creature went limp. I was about to haul him off, but Vi, being a farmer's wife and knowledgeable about such matters cried, "No, let him finish it off, it would be worse to leave it half-dead." Its eyes were glazing already, poor little thing but Bounty was as proud as a lion! His six inch tail wasn't just upright, it curved over towards his back. Head held high he trotted for at least a mile back to the car, still carrying the rabbit.

"Drop it!" I commanded hopefully.

"NO WAY!" his body language replied.

"How are we going to catch him?" called Vi frantically after we had chased him around and around the field for a quarter of an hour. Then she had an inspiration. "Try 'the kitchen'," she said.

"BOUNTY!" I thundered, "Do you want to go in the kitchen?" How he thought he could be transported the fifteen to twenty miles or so home, I don't know but it worked! He stood still and thankfully I clipped on the lead and led him to the car. He wouldn't release his hold on the rabbit, though, growling and wagging his tail at the same time, indicating "I know you're supposed to be the boss, but JUST DON'T TRY ANYTHING!" So dog and corpse got into his cardboard box on the back seat.

As we drove along a foul smell pervaded the car. "Oh YUK!" I said, glancing in the rear view mirror at the happy, bloodstained little face, "He's EATING it!"

We wanted to stop at a garden centre on the way home and parked in a far corner of their car park so no-one would see our killer dog. I took him out to stretch his legs while Vi surreptitiously retrieved the remains of the mangled corpse, placing it in a plastic bag and dumping it in a waste bin. He sniffed around for it when he got back in, but was soon asleep, tired after his excitement.

Perhaps it sounds callous allowing a pet dog to catch a rabbit but it was purely instinct on his part. As I've mentioned, his parents are both working Jack Russells and go out with the foxhounds each winter. It wasn't what I had in mind for HIM though and decided to channel his instincts into less harmful outlets, playing with him more than ever for the next few weeks.

Chapter 4

Problems

Every night, when Bounty was still only a few months old, I would put him to bed in the kitchen at about 8.30pm and sneak into my bedroom where I had concealed chocolate biscuits, feasting myself without disappointing him or spoiling his teeth - and also having a bit of peace! (All these extra walks increased my appetite.) He had outgrown several cardboard boxes as well as his first dog bed by now, and measured thirteen inches to the shoulder, so I bought a larger dog bed. That is something else the uninitiated (myself!) did not realise - how much everything costs. He had got through three collars and five leads at six months, mainly through chewing leads or starting off at a gallop. He always went to bed reluctantly and I loved him dearly by this time, even though he still tired me out. He tolerated me quite well, too, but was still the boss.

Anyhow, my resolve had weakened and one night, instead of putting him in the kitchen I put his bed in my room. He couldn't believe his eyes and thought this was great! Early next morning around 1.00am I suddenly felt a weight on my legs. His bed was rejected from then on and mine became his - only ever on TOP of the clothes, I hasten to add. He is quite content with that.

Sometimes he asked to go out in the early hours and I would stumble to the back door in the dark like a zombie to let him into the garden. One particular night though, he woke me and didn't want to go out but sniffed around the bungalow, then came back to bed, obviously ill at ease about something, sitting up and making no attempt to go back to sleep. Suddenly there was a loud bang and a flash from the electric point at the foot of my bed. A bare wire had blown a fuse and he must have sensed it. It gave him a terrible fright, poor little soul and he came shivering to my arms, where I held him tight. I showed him the bare wire (having first unplugged it) and let him sniff the source of his fright to help him understand that it was all over. At last we settled down again, but I felt very proud of my little protector!

His puppy coat was almost smooth in those early days. He is now broken-coated, but that first winter he felt the cold and shivered when we were out in a wind. We don't get much snow in the south, but there was a light fall that year, so I decided I would make him a little jacket. I am certainly no needlewoman, but I cut the sleeve from an old sheepskin coat, shaped and sewed it in front to make a hole for his head and fastened a canvas belt around his middle like a horse's girth. He liked it from the start and trotted out proudly on his walks, feeling the cold no longer. He was growing so fast it would have been an expensive waste to buy a new one.

My dog was becoming a great little character, making detours through puddles like a mischievous child, 'helping' me in the garden by digging holes and running off with the watering can, taking clothes out of the washing machine when I was trying to fill it, and if he thought he had missed anything, ran around to see what it was with a "What? What? What?" expression on his face. His yawn sounded like an iron gate with a rusty hinge, and when I was talking on the telephone performed all sorts of antics such as chewing my foot or climbing on my head, to try and distract me. You could see him thinking, "Poor soul, talking to herself. I must make her snap out of it!" He was a very good watch-dog, barking loudly at callers and the postman. One day that summer, a letter came from the National Trust and he barked furiously as usual. In it, they said they would be pleased to sell my first novel and I was delighted at the news. W.H. Smith, John Menzies and Waterstones were already selling it, but the National Trust was my 'make or break' factor. "Whoopee, Bounty - we've cracked it!" I yelled, picking him up and hugging him, and as it has turned out, the National Trust has sold more copies for me than anyone.

On the rare occasions when I went out on my own I only had to say, "Good boy, stay there and look after the house," and he'd flop down in the hall, looking soulful but making no attempt to come. As I passed the bay window, a little white face with brown ears and eye patches would appear and gaze after me, eyes pleading ... I hated going out! So much so, that it made me give up something I had been doing for twenty years and more. I had undertaken voluntary work at a club at Christchurch Hospital, but recently hurt my shoulder and arm while lifting, and it was troubling me quite a lot. I was told to rest it and 'take things easier' but still continued to attend - and also run the gauntlet of Bounty's soulful gaze. I was driving there one Monday evening, feeling twinges from my shoulder when I suddenly thought, "I don't HAVE to do this!" It came to me, that for the past twenty years or so I had always done what was expected of me. Aware of the years accelerating like time-lapse pictures of speeding clouds, I resolved to fulfil some of my OWN ambitions while I was still able and before creeping arthritis really took a hold. So later that week, I spoke to the club leader and asked if he minded me taking a sabbatical. To my surprise he agreed without looking annoyed (no-one is indispensable!) and the following Monday I said happily to Bounty, "I'm not going out tonight!" and we settled down for a pleasant evening together.

★ ★ ★

I was in the garden one Sunday when I saw Bounty eating grass again, which he seemed to do more than most dogs. (Not enough roughage in his food, I have since been told). As was to be expected, he was sick but fell over during his retching, and shivered. I had a bad fright and rang the Vet. Of course, being Sunday a different, emergency vet about five miles away was on call. I needed someone to hold Bounty while I drove there so asked Peg next door if she would come with me. It was 10.00pm by then, but, bless her, she came without hesitation and held the little fellow in her arms, wrapped in a towel, until we arrived. The Vet asked me to put my dog on the examination table, so I unwrapped him, placing him carefully on its surface. Released, Bounty leaped up and bounced around, full of life!

"Er - what seems to be the trouble?" asked the Vet, looking at me strangely. I told him and he began to examine the patient, deftly inserting the thermometer. Bounty didn't like that!

"Yow!" yelled the vet, smacking him on the nose, "He bit me!" A slightly raised temperature and tummy upset was diagnosed and he injected a dose of antibiotics which cost me £27.00. I think I paid for treatment for HIS bite, as well!

Next day, Bounty was fine, so I breathed a sigh of relief. However could I have entertained the thought of sending him back to the kennels?

Our relationship was cemented even more firmly on the night of the spectacular electric storm in July 1991. Its like had not been seen for many a year. I had, up until then been apprehensive of thunder and lightning, but with my 'young man' to protect me I had no fears, and at 2.00am we sat on the back doorstep together watching the 'heavenly fireworks', my arm holding him close. He was fascinated and not at all scared, barking at the first clap of thunder as though it was a particularly noisy lorry. Yes, I felt well protected now!

His 'vocabulary' increased daily. If I asked, "Where's your big bone?" he would trot around until he found it (usually in my bedroom) pointing to it with his nose. An unwanted treat would be buried in the garden. He was funny, not concealing it if he knew I was watching but once it was hidden and buried he would re-appear with dirty whiskers and beard, then I would ask, "Where is it?" and he would promptly run and show me! It was strange, he understood everything except, "Come here!" and this was something he was determined not to recognise. I sometimes wished there was a Telephone Helpline for dog owners with problems, but as I didn't know of one, I decided Dog Training Classes might be the answer.

Chapter 5

Training

There was a puppy training class starting in a hall not too far away, so we enroled. Bounty loved meeting dogs and it was always difficult to get him to leave them when we were out walking. He was better off the lead than on, pulling frantically when restrained, so these, plus 'COME' were the main problems I wanted to correct.

On the first night we had to attend without our dogs. There were eleven of us plus three trainers. They explained the pro's and con's of different types of leads and collars, then one of them said, "I have a question for you ... 'What is a dog?'"

The person next to me said hesitantly, "A faithful friend and companion...?"

"A dog is a descendant of a wolf," he corrected. "It is naturally a pack animal and once you realise that, you will understand why they behave as they do. There are dominant ones who work their way up through the pecking order to be leader of the pack and there are the underdogs. I expect you know by now which category YOUR particular pup comes under. If you let them be dominant at this age they will be insecure and ill-mannered. YOU are the boss and must let them see you are. You don't have to be cruel - I don't believe in physical punishment, it can all be done by tone of voice." All good, sound stuff so far.

The next week we turned up with our dogs. Bounty thought it was great and started making eyes at a rough collie, twice his size that took his fancy.

I was reprimanded in our first session as I had been trying to persuade Bounty to come by calling, "Here Bounty, good boy!" and as usual he was ignoring me.

"No," said the trainer firmly, "You're confusing him. He's NOT a good boy if he doesn't come. You are praising him for standing still.

Say very positively, 'Bounty, COME!' It takes time and practice, but persevere."

We also did 'walking to heel' with Bounty straining at the leash. It was aggravating, he walked close to me in the open country without any trouble but in town it was different.

"Get your dog's attention," called the trainer - not easy when my Jack Russell pup was so far down and I so tall - "and don't let him PULL. Keep the lead short, let it go slack, then give it a little jerk. Keep on doing that, and he'll soon learn."

Another thing we were told was 'not to give two commands when we meant only one, for example, 'sit down', which to a dog is two separate actions, 'sit' and 'down'. It was all very logical when you thought about it.

Bounty really enjoyed going to 'school' every week and it was a pleasure to see all the pups improving. We were a mixed bunch - German Shepherds, Boxers, Rough Collies, a Labrador, a Golden Retriever, a Rotweiler (whose handler was five foot nothing and weighed about seven stone, less than the dog I should think!) and my little Jack Russell - but surprisingly they all got on very well together. Bounty had a 'very good' for his 'sit', but actually my great niece Emma who was twelve taught him that in about ten minutes, so I couldn't claim any credit. He now uses the 'sit' to his own advantage, associating it with food as Emma rewarded him with tit-bits. He sits in front of me if he feels like a snack when we are out, gazing up at me tremulously in case I have forgotten to bring his Pedigree Complete Formula biscuits with me. (His favourite, except he only likes the variety for females with pups!) Another trick is to gaze at the mantelpiece where I keep his 'Beef Smackos'. "What is it, love?" I ask, pretending not to understand, so he looks pointedly at the mantelpiece again then back into my eyes. Of course, such intelligence has to be rewarded!

Unfortunately, but quite naturally around this time, Bounty entered what the Vet called 'a phase' - he became amorous and grabbed anything that moved, human feet, legs, handbags and usually the wrong end of dogs - German Shepherd's heads for preference! It was embarrassing and often difficult to prise him off. On one occasion, before I realised what was happening he grabbed an elderly man by the leg in the recreation ground. The poor old chap looked most surprised as I apologized profusely. Another dog-walker, seeing what had happened muttered, "He probably hasn't had such a thrill for years!"

Scent played a very important part around this time and when one of the farmworker's dogs was in season, Bounty sat and howled frustratedly at being kept away from her - and he was only nine months old!

Apart from that, all was going very well with the training classes until we had a two week break for the trainers' annual refresher course.

"Keep up your homework," they said, "and we'll see you in two weeks time," but as things turned out, for Bounty that was not to be...

Chapter 6

Favourite Walks

We have many favourite walks: the local Recreation Ground and Alexandra Park to hob-knob with his chums, the moors at Talbot Heath, Broadstone Recreation Ground which includes heath and woodland as well as playing fields, Delph Woods, Branksome Chine, Wareham Forest, Redhill Common (on a Saturday morning on our way to Margaret and Joe's for coffee) but I think one of Bounty's favourites overlooks Corfe Castle in the Purbecks. Wind ruffles his long eyebrows - they rival those of Dennis Healey - and he tears around, nose down, snuffling happily after rabbits.

In the wooded walks I see him disappearing in one direction only to reappear from quite another, almost immediately - it's rather uncanny, and people might be forgiven for assuming there were two dogs instead of one.

When he was small I had a real dread of losing him down a hole. The kennel man had warned me, if you remember, that Jack Russells couldn't be stopped, it was their natural instinct so from an early age I got him accustomed to being gently hauled backwards by his tail, just in case! Apparently Jack Russells should have a six inch tail for this very purpose, but fortunately so far, and most unusually, he has never shown any wish to go underground.

From the West Street car park in Corfe Castle, an often unnoticed footpath leads away across a couple of fields, through some trees and out on to the Common. Visitors more often than not head for the splendid ruins of the castle and miss this hidden part of Dorset, which has hardly changed in centuries. I often walked there before the advent of Bounty, but in his company it was even more pleasant.

Where the footpath meets the Common there is an ancient single-arched stone footbridge over the clear waters of the brook. Its source is a spring in the pond at Blashenwell Farm which dates back to

Domesday Book. The Common covers many acres and is crossed by the road to Kingston on the hill. Ponies and donkeys graze there while rabbits lead dogs a merry chase before escaping into tangles of brambles. The close-cropped turf is full of wild thyme and small creeping wild flowers bonsai'd from being grazed through countless centuries. Late spring brings many wild orchis's to hidden, secluded glades concealed from the main path by boggy ground. It is altogether a delightful place and it goes without saying that Bounty is always pleased when he discovers Corfe is our destination.

We usually return by way of West Street because there is nearly always a stall outside one of the houses, selling plants, fruit, garden produce and homemade marmalade. A tin sits on top to put your money in and you serve yourself, taking change if needed - the tin is never locked! Stone cottages along the way could have come straight from the lid of a chocolate box - crooked windows, stone roofs and walls with gardens and borders looking as cottage gardens ought to look. There is a Daisy Cottage, a Russet Cottage and a Furzemans House with worn doorstep from the tread of feet throughout the years, while another has entwined initials over the lintel with the date 1741.

Another place he really loves is a deserted beach, charging along like a mad thing, splashing through the shallows, rolling on ancient fish and crunching dead crabs, shells and all! His mouth is so close to the ground that they are gone before I can stop him. Luckily he loves the water, so the fishy smell soon washes off.

His delight in finding he could swim came one day in the upper reaches of the Bourne stream that gives Bournemouth its name. It rises in the moors near Wallisdown, runs under a railway embankment near Coy Pond then emerges into two and a half miles of gardens extending all the way to the sea at Bournemouth. Like Branksome Chine, they are intersected by roads which need care and in all but the two gardens nearest the sea, dogs are allowed off the lead.

He loves to race along the bed of a brook and this time unexpectedly came to a deeper pool, only to find he was swimming - oh joy! Back and forth he went, ecstatically emerging to look like one of his smooth-haired cousins. People say to me, "He's lovely and white, he must be difficult to keep clean," but he hates being dirty and washes his paws like a cat. With his now frequent swims in rivers, streams and the sea his coat is usually whiter than white.

When he was just a pup, about four months old, Joan and I took him across to Shell Bay on the Sandbanks chain ferry. He is a proper sea-dog, almost as though he knows he is named after the sixteenth century Poole merchant ship which gave my first novel its title, and which was fired on by the gunners of Brownsea Castle near this very place. He races up to the top deck, looking over the rail and standing on his hind legs, sniffing the sea breeze like a true 'old salt'.

On this occasion, Joan and I walked along the beautiful wide sweeping beach which stretches some three miles to the pretty little village of Studland, once the haunt of pirates. Bounty loved it, quartering the ground back and forth, exploring the dunes, beach and sea. We had a good pub lunch at the Bankes Arms in Studland (they admit dogs) then walked back to the ferry. I attempted to carry him in case he was tired but he wriggled to be put down again. Well, WE had walked about six miles, so it was anybody's guess how many HE had covered, and that evening I read in a Jack Russell handbook, 'When your puppy is three to four months old you can begin taking him for short walks'!!

I must admit, I felt a little stiff myself, as there had been a cold wind - it was February, so that evening took a bath instead of a shower. As I finished and stood up to let the water out, Bounty was most intrigued, leaning over, watching it gurgling down the waste pipe. Then suddenly he slipped - and with a splosh there were two of us in the bath! This was great fun, he thought, and splashed around merrily, jumping out and running wetly around the house before I could don my bath robe and catch him! He showed no ill-effects whatsoever after his long walk. Perhaps the bath did him good, too!

When he was a few months older, we did the walk to Studland again. It was summer then and John, Joan's husband came with us. We once again had lunch at the Bankes Arms but this time sat in the pub garden with its views over Studland bay to Old Harry Rocks. Mundays Tavern, a well-known haunt of pirates and vagabonds in Elizabethan times was very near this site, but now there were only people enjoying the fine weather, the view and the pub food. Leaving

John and Bounty guarding our table, Joan and I went to get our refreshments. We were carrying them out, when I said to Joan, "Oh, John has moved tables," then saw it wasn't him at all - or was it Bounty, but the Jack Russell I had seen was how he would look when he was grown up! It was really odd, like seeing into the future - the same markings, similar expression, long legs, broken coat! Of course, when we had eaten we went over and spoke to the owners, a young couple from Reading who said they often drove to Purbeck for the weekend. Their dog loved it, too they told us. He was friendly with people, they said, but not other dogs so we couldn't show Bounty in close-up how he would look in years to come.

Baiter is an area of grassy, reclaimed land at the edge of Poole Harbour. In bygone days it was the site of a windmill, isolation hospital and gunpowder store. Its southern shores give extensive views over the islands in the harbour with the Purbeck hills beyond, while Corfe Castle nestles in its gap in the chalk downland range - yes, Baiter is an ideal place for a walk. Bounty loves to scatter the flocks of gulls that settle in the squidgy grass - it always seems to be wet underfoot - enjoying mad dashes through the puddles and raising rainbows of spray. Usually there are other dogs to romp with and it is a joy to see them, running free, chasing each other and rolling in the grass without being a nuisance to anyone. How I pity poor city dogs that can never experience this freedom.

★ ★ ★

When we go to the shops at Parkstone, he enlivens the walk through residential streets by looking for cats, remembering every house where he even saw a WHISKER once! After all, the cat MIGHT reappear! There is one house where the cat must have been very wicked, because it has TURNED TO STONE! Bounty stands on his hind legs, looking over the wall with horrible fascination as the stone cat, unmoving, glares back at him.

During the last hundred yards or so of our evening walk, he went through a phase of finding a cigarette packet, crisp bag or scrap of paper to carry home. Once inside the gate I let him off the lead and that was the signal for the 'Grand National' to begin. I have three irregularly shaped beds of heather in the front lawn, dating back to 'when I was a gardener' last year. Plants flower throughout the year in rotation, or else have multi-coloured foliage and people used to stop and admire them. There is one spreading heather called 'Springwood White' which was the favourite flopping down place in the evening rubbish collection. Of course, in the game I had to try and get it from him, whereupon he raced around and around the garden taking the 'fences' like Red Rum in his prime, stopping now and again just beyond my reach to get his breath, then off he went again. Well - as Joan once said, 'It's his home too!' At least the heather is fairly resilient.

★ ★ ★

A dog owner who lives nearby told me he walks his dog at 6.00am in the then deserted car park of the Trading Estate on the hill. They often meet a fox that obviously lives there. It usually takes no notice of them, but one day apparently wanted to show them something. The man followed the vixen and she proudly displayed to him her six cubs.

I have seen urban foxes in the winter on our evening walk around the block, at first mistaking them for cats until their silhouette gave them away. I don't know how they manage to survive as we have 'wheelie bins' which are virtually fox-proof.

One day, Betty Smith called me round to her house where we could see a distressed vixen lying in the long grass of her elderly neighbour's garden. We called the Animal Ambulance who speedily collected it, but said it was in a very sorry, emaciated state and full of mange so would have to be put down.

I once heard a weird, unearthly screeching at night, not eight feet from my bedroom window. Looking out, I saw a beautiful, long-legged fox playing with something on the lawn, tossing it in the air in the moonlight. Next morning - oh horrors! - there were small pieces of hedgehog skin on the grass!

★ ★ ★

Another walk he used to enjoy was through Wareham Forest, chasing squirrels and bounding along happily until one day, in the disconcerting manner dogs have, he kept staring at things I couldn't see ... His tail drooped and he ran a few paces, crouching low then stopped, staring again at 'nothing'.

"What is it?" I asked, listening, but couldn't hear anything other than the gentle sighing of the wind in the pines. "Shall we go back then?" I said, and most unusually he was relieved to turn around, scuttling along and glancing over his shoulder. It really was eerie. I tried the same walk again a couple of weeks later and his behaviour was still as peculiar.

Now I have heard since that some months previously a little Jack Russell had been lost, probably down a foxhole in Wareham Forest and despite an extensive search was never found. Had Bounty sensed a 'restless spirit' I wonder?

Chapter 7

Summer Holidays

I cancelled my trip to my cousin in Yorkshire which was to have taken place in June, as Bounty was too young to be left, and in any case I would have dreaded parting from him. We contented ourselves with day outings - after all, we lived on the south coast of England with the New Forest only half an hour away by car and surrounded by the beautiful countryside of Dorset, and, however fond I am of my cousins, why leave for pastures new?

My neighbour Dave on the opposite side to Peg had two small boys. They were fascinated by Bounty and were always calling to him through the gate. One day, I found them dropping gravel for him between the wrought iron bars. "Oh, don't do that please," I cried, "he might eat it and be killed!"

"Never mind", said the youngest (who was just four) innocently, "If it did, I would buy you another one." How was I to explain there could never BE another Bounty?

A few days later their father told me they were all going on holiday, and asked if I would look after their tortoises.

"Of course," I said, being neighbourly.

"I'll bring them around last thing on Friday," he said, "Thanks."

"Oh, but - wouldn't it be better if I went to your house to feed them?" I asked dubiously.

"No, they're valuable," he said, "I wouldn't want them unsupervised."

"But what about Bounty?"

"They won't worry about him, they'll go into their shells," he said. That wasn't quite what I meant, but I agreed with some trepidation. Friday evening came and Dave arrived with four hinged boards, about a foot high which formed their run (if a tortoise exercise area can be called a 'run') and a little house for the creatures to sleep in.

"Here's their cucumber and lettuce," he said holding up a Sainsbury's carrier bag, "and we'll be back in a week's time."

Bounty had been in the kitchen while all this was going on, and I cautiously opened the door to see what would happen. He shot out, an outraged ball of white fur, barking furiously.

"COME HERE!" I yelled and made a grab at him, bundling the indignant form back into the kitchen where his frustrated yapping rattled the windows. "What's to do?" I muttered frantically, "I've got these creatures for a week and I can't ban Bounty from the garden!" Then I espied a roll of wire netting I'd bought to put along the front hedge and cut a couple of pieces from it, placing them over the bewildered tortoises.

Carefully I let Bounty out again. He dashed straight over to them and stuck his head under the wire, missing one of their noses by millimetres! Back into the kitchen he was banished while I collected hammer and nails and made them a see-through roof. This time, Bounty leapt on top of it, growling at the 'walking Cornish pasties' in frustration, trying to tear at the wire with his teeth. It was quite a week! He was fascinated, especially when they ate, but I didn't dare leave him unattended in the garden until Dave and his family returned.

★ ★ ★

Usually at some time in the school holidays my two great-nieces, Emma and Laura stay with me and this year was to be no different. They both adore Bounty, and there was much giggling when they went to bed. Peeping around the door I found the two girls and Bounty completely submerged under a wriggling duvet! He had never had anyone to stay overnight before and thought it was great fun! I was abandoned and felt quite lonely, but in the early hours the little fellow appeared on my bed with a "Sorry mum, just thought I ought to keep an eye on them, y'know!" expression.

Eventually we all managed somehow to get a little sleep that first night, which was just as well as we were going to the New Forest Show at Brockenhurst next day.

The morning dawned bright and sunny and we set off in high spirits, accompanied by Joan. As Bounty had to be on the lead in the showground we decided to have a break at Burley in the Forest to give him a chance to run free. Leaving the car at Castle Hill we walked the mile or so through woodland glades along the rough track to Burley. We passed a pond covered in duck-weed but Bounty hadn't learned from his escapade at Worth Matravers and splashed straight into it, emerging with a look of surprise, and duck-weed in his long eyebrows. Still, the day was warm and getting hotter so it didn't do him any harm. Deer melted silently into the background, unnoticed, as he was having the whale of a time sniffing trails and running back to make sure we were all there. Emma, who was twelve and like a long-legged deer herself ran races with him and he scampered along like a tiny greyhound, determined to beat her.

We found a cafe at Burley that didn't mind dogs and sat outside at a table facing the road. Bounty was as good as gold, used to Joan and I having breaks for coffee and scones on our walks, but not so three free-ranging donkeys which strolled up and joined us, knocking over crockery and trying to steal the sugar, to squeals of delight from the girls.

Eventually, we reached the showground. There was an awful lot to see; ponies in hand, jumping, cattle, carriages, a dog show, hundreds of stalls, a craft marquee, a funfair - and the day grew hotter. We queued for the loos, then for food which we ate sitting in the shade of an oak, not forgetting plenty of water for Bounty which I squirted from a Spanish wineskin. It is very easy to carry and caused amusement to onlookers as he drank from it like a veteran Spaniard! Then we queued for ice-cream, had goes on the funfair then queued in the car part to get out - altogether a rather exhausting day.

Next morning we were up early again as we were travelling by car to the Isle of Wight. The ever-resilient Joan came with us again (to ensure fair play for Bounty!). I couldn't believe how well-behaved he was, travelling on the ferry, being driven around the island and then, the highlight of our trip, a visit to Blackgang Chine. It is a lovely place for children, with life-sized models grouped strategically throughout the cliffside park. There were dinosaurs, a Western town complete with hill-billy train, a Wells Fargo bank, stage coach, stores, Indian wigwams, loads of wild animals, a fairytale castle and many other sights to delight the hearts of children. We took Bounty into the Hall of Mirrors and laughed until we were helpless at our long necks, short legs, fat bodies and elongated arms! We took plenty of 'touristy' photographs and, not to be outdone, Bounty posed for his behind a cut-out of a gorilla body with a hole for his face.

Before we left, Laura wanted to go to the loo, so leaving Bounty with Joan and Emma I took her there. We were gone for about fifteen minutes by the time I found it and she had a go at finding her way through the Maze, but had arranged to meet the others by the gorilla so that was no problem. Emma was waiting, looking mischievous and obviously trying to detain me, then all was revealed a few minutes later when Joan and Bounty reappeared.

"Got it?" whispered Emma. Joan nodded secretively and held out a carrier bag to me.

"What's this?" I asked curiously.

"Have a look!" said Joan. Opening the bag carefully I found a tee-shirt with Bounty's photo printed on it and the inscription, 'Love me - love my dog'.

"A little thank-you," said Joan with a grin.

I felt tears pricking my eyelids. "What a lovely surprise!" I mumbled gratefully, "I shall wear this with pride!"

It had been a lovely day and once again the little fellow had been SO good, thoroughly enjoying his outing. I must admit, though, we all slept extremely well that night.

Chapter 8

Bounty Gets Lost

In the long summer evenings, we often walked through Branksome Chine. This is a beautiful natural area of mainly pinewoods with beech, oak, sycamore and holly stretching some two miles to the sea. Through it runs a little stream, the bed and banks of which were faced with stone by Welsh miners during the Depression of the 1930's. As it nears the sea, the area opens out into a wide ravine, or 'chine' to give it its local name. However, the walk has two disadvantages - the woods are unfenced for the main part, and are intersected by roads.

On this particular fateful evening, Bounty was off the lead as usual, investigating every scent and tree. Sunlight glinted through the leaves and occasional squirrels leapt from bough to bough. A man with a Labrador gazed up at them, saying wryly, "Those chaps have a hard time of it. No sooner do they come down than they're chased up again!" One paused halfway up a tree and just out of reach, scolding us. Then a lady came by, her spaniel skulking along the bed of the stream. "It's all right," she said, "He's trying to throw the Red Indians off his trail!"

I walked on towards the sea, smiling to myself at the eccentricities of dog-owners, when suddenly Bounty shot up the pine-needle covered side of the ravine - another squirrel, I assumed and waited. It was very quiet. I grew apprehensive.

"Bounty, COME!" I called loudly. Nothing! I shouted his name, over and over again and searched through the undergrowth. Was he trapped somewhere? Had he fallen and hit his head? Could he hear me? Then I began to run, calling as I went but there was still no sign of him and I could feel my heartbeat quicken apprehensively. I met other people walking their dogs. "Have you seen a little white Jack Russell with brown ears?" I asked desperately.

"No, sorry," they replied. There was noisy traffic on the road on either side of the woods, and I ran on, dreading a screech of brakes and a sickening 'thump'.

I met more people. "Have you seen a little Jack Russell?" I asked again, even more fearfully, but they hadn't. They did enquire, though, seeing my agitation how they could get in touch with me if they found him.

"My telephone number is on his collar," I told them, "and there's an answerphone connected if I'm still not home."

They muttered something sympathetic about him turning up soon, and I left them, hurrying out of the woods and on to the road, searching and calling until I was hoarse. Still nothing! My heart felt like lead. What would I do without him? My mind was going in circles, anticipating the worst and imagining my empty home. Would I get another dog, and if so, would it be a Jack Russell?

Back into the woods I went, still traversing the paths back and forth, calling his name. Half an hour passed. What should I do - 'phone the Police? It was no good ringing Joan to come and help, she was away. I felt numb and very much alone.

Then a young man came towards me. I recognised him as one I had seen earlier in my search. He gave me a wave. "I think we have your dog!" he called.

"Oh THANK you!" I cried with relief and ran, gasping in the direction from which he had come. As I rounded the corner I saw his girl friend, crouched down, and with great difficulty holding a wriggling Bounty!

"He was chasing after a female in season!" she told me, grinning. And him only eleven months old!

I thought the little lost waif would be delighted to see me - but no, I'd spoilt his fun and he was most disgruntled - there wasn't even a wag from his tail!

Thanking the couple profusely, I clipped the lead firmly to his collar.

"Right, THAT'S IT, young man," I said, looking my pup in the eye, "I'm not going through THAT again, YOU are off to the Vet next week - it's FOR YOUR OWN GOOD!"

Chapter 9

The Operation

I made an appointment with the Vet for the following Tuesday, but I kept having doubts - was I doing the correct thing? He was such a lovely little dog, it didn't seem right somehow to 'spoil' him. I had heard tales of dogs' personalities changing after being neutered; would his change for the worse?

Once before, on the banks of the river Stour at Christchurch he ran away, but I assumed then he had panicked. Perhaps he had been lovelorn then, too?

As usual, I discussed it with Joan who had been horrified at the thought of me losing him. Was it wrong to deny him the chance of being a father, I asked her.

"Well," she said sensibly, "if he WAS, you'd only worry about the pups and if they were going to good homes."

"You're right, and anyhow," I said with a sly grin, "we don't know if he actually CAUGHT that female in the woods, do we?" (I think she was a spaniel, from what the girl described so I keep on the lookout for strange cross-breeds in that district!)

Nevertheless, that weekend I kept having feelings of remorse. Bounty had extra-special walks, ON the lead of course, just in case he tried for a final fling, plus his favourite food and treats to cover my 'guilt'.

When I made the appointment I was told Bounty must have nothing to eat after 7.30 in the evening, so at 6.45pm I gave him his dinner. He turned up his nose although it was his favourite tripe and sat in the armchair, watching 'Country Ways' on TV. I offered it to him again at 7.15pm, but still he wasn't interested so at 7.30pm I took it away. Of course, at 8.00pm he was asking, "Where's my dinner?" I felt awful!

Next day we drove to the Vet's. All unsuspecting, he trotted in happily and we took our turn in the waiting room.

"It's for the best," I told him, but as soon as were called into the treatment room he 'smelt a rat' and started to shiver. As he was having his injection he pushed his little head under my armpit, asking to be saved, and it crossed my mind how truly awful it must be to have a dog put to sleep - a thought which often haunts me. I knew I would be getting mine back at 4.30pm the same day, but I still felt I was abandoning him in this unknown place, and amongst strangers.

He soon became 'wobbly' and the Vet's assistant took him through to the operating room. I left blindly, feeling tears oozing from my eyelids. Vi had come with me for moral support, and we drove to Bournemouth to go in all the shops that banned dogs.

To take our minds off things, we had coffee in a restaurant but unusually for me I couldn't eat a thing, my appetite had gone.

4.30pm couldn't come soon enough. Vi took me back to the Vet's but there wasn't room to park so dropped me off to collect the patient while she drove around the block.

The Vet was a locum but I had every confidence in him. He was obviously kind and caring - you wouldn't find HIM smacking Bounty on the nose!

My sleepy little dog was carried out of the recovery room and placed on the table. The Vet examined him saying, "A lovely job - even though I say so myself - and no problems! Bring him back in ten days and I'll take the stitches out."

Carefully I carried Bounty to the car with his little operation area all shaven. Vi had found a car space by then and drove us home. He slept a lot, but went out for 'tiddles' last thing, which he performed standing on four legs, looking bewildered. I was reminded of the time when he first learned to lift his leg after puppy squatting. He had a rough idea what to do, but sometimes lifted the wrong leg, aiming AWAY from his target until he got the hang of it!

I placed his seldom used, only in the daytime nowadays, bed on the floor of my room that night, so he wouldn't strain his stitches by jumping up on my bed, and he slept soundly. Next morning he was still rather wobbly, but by 2.30pm was out with me in the garden, 'helping' by digging a hole!

We were careful for the next ten days, not too much running and

The Operation

avoiding muddy water with possible infection, then I took him back to have his stitches removed.

In case the car park was full again I parked nearby and we walked the rest of the way. Bounty trotted confidently by my side, interested in everything as usual. We crossed the Vet's car park (which was empty, of course!) and approached the surgery. A man was delivering goods and, seeing Bounty called, "He's a tough 'un! My dog has to be DRAGGED in!"

Whether Bounty understood him or not, he suddenly realised where he was and hung back. I lifted him up and felt his little body trembling.

"It's all right, love," I consoled him, "I'm not leaving you this time," and then it was our turn to go in.

The Vet, having removed the two little stitches pronounced everything was satisfactory, and Bounty couldn't get out quickly enough!

★ ★ ★

Looking back, I have never regretted taking that step. It has made him a much more affectionate little fellow. (He is lying on my feet as I write and has just removed by socks, one by one). He checks on my whereabouts, following me from room to room. I see a movement, look up and there he is, head cocked saying, "Can I help?" He leaves other dogs without any hassle and (mostly!) comes when he is called - altogether a pleasure and a joy to live with - and how my life was changing!

Chapter 10

Bounty's Friends

Bounty loved Joan and husband John of course. Vi and Jim, also my great nieces and nephews Emma, Laura, Paul and Lawrence. I only have to mention their names and the little dog cocks his little head on one side expectantly. Sometimes I test him when they are with me and say, "Where's Emma?" He looks at her, then at me as if to say, "Are you daft, she's over there!"

Another friend is a retired schoolteacher whose garden backs on to mine. She is a real animal lover, taking in stray dogs, cats, rabbits and tortoises. One of her terriers lived to be twenty five years of age! Bounty always makes a fuss of her and she loves his little beard, saying she can never resist stroking it.

One of his passions is for tissues and he goes to great lengths to seek them out. Two gentle paws prod my thigh while a little nose snuffles in the depths of my pocket, withdrawing one neatly. Last week I was chatting to a friend in the street and Bounty, thinking we had gone on long enough, started poking around UNDER the old 'dog-walking' raincoat I was wearing. How did he know there was a hole in the pocket? His head emerged like a triumphant magician, holding a tissue in his teeth. One day, he even managed to unzip Vi's handbag when she left it unattended on the floor and quietly removed one of hers, happily shredding it on the carpet. He used to eat them when he was younger and someone remarked, "Hmm, internal toilet paper—now that's different!"

Another time I was in my bedroom and must have left the bathroom door open. A strange noise came from the hall and looking out, I saw Bounty doing an 'Andrex Ad' with great glee all around the house, while the toilet roll unravelled behind him.

To get back to his friends, Peg and husband Doug next door are certainly in that category. If he sees them going out, he barks furiously from his perch on the back of an armchair in the window while at the same time wagging his tail to show he's not angry. They often look after their daughter's dog, Kelpie, and he and Bounty have great conversations through the hedge.

Another couple of friends are the 'Two Betty's'. Along with myself, they have probably resided the longest in my road, both being there when I was a child. (I was born in this bungalow and have lived here all my life). They are both pensioners and Bounty and I regularly take them by car to their club on Bournemouth Road, collecting them again afterwards. Betty Smith's husband Ted died just before I had Bounty and Bet Fry is also a widow.

My pup was barely seven weeks old in November 1990 when I came home from the farm one Sunday and parked outside my house. Seeing Betty Smith at her door saying goodbye to Bet Fry who lives across the road I said, "I must introduce you to Betty, little one." Locking the car, I walked three doors away to her house where we chatted at her gate for a few mintues as she admired my new offspring.

"Mustn't keep him out in the cold too long," I said eventually and took him home. Glancing down at my front door (the bungalow is on the side of a hill and in a hollow) I saw immediately that something was wrong - oh horrors! No-one should have been at home, but a gaping void stood in place of the strong white door! Clutching Bounty to me tightly I entered in some trepidation. The drawers in my bedroom were open , but all the other rooms were intact and NOTHING had been taken! The intruder may have been disturbed, or else was after money which I NEVER keep in the house. Or I like to think perhaps he had seen the error of his ways, as I have a postcard motto pinned to the mirror in my bedroom which reads, 'Today is the first day of the rest of your life'!

Anyhow, the two Betty's became firm favourites with my little dog. We have a standing invitation to coffee with Betty Smith, and I only have to say to Bounty, "Shall we go and see Betty?" and he jumps around with excitment and runs to her gate.

His best doggie friend is, of course Sharp and they play a (to humans) silly game for hours, where Bounty gets under a chair for safety and they playbite each other, slapping paws in mock fights like a couple of mad March hares. Sharp, being a working collie consistently tries to 'herd' Bounty when they are out together, but the little fellow after much practice has cleverly learned to dodge him.

We meet other friends in the Recreation ground, a regular exercise area for dogs around the perimeter of the football pitches, most of their owners complete with 'poop scoops' and plastic bags. The company he enjoys best is that of two lively little Lancashire Heelers and their staid companion, an elderly Old English Sheepdog. The little ones have mad races together, while the elderly dog watches them anxiously, remembering her youth.

Then there are the Alexandra Park friends. The park lies behind the shops in Upper Parkstone and is of an irregular shape—a wild park, hilly, with grass and trees and a fenced-off childrens playground. Best of all it has a population of squirrels and NO CYCLING, so dogs are safe to run free as the park is fenced with three unobtrusive exits into fairly quiet roads. The squirrels here travel up and down the trees like yo-yo's as the park isn't very big and most walkers complete two or three circuits. Bounty's largest friend is Amy a lolloppy, friendly Old English Sheepdog with a beard that picks up mud. Her owner is always cautioning people to mind their clothes as Amy likes to speak to everyone and be admired. Then there is Popeye, a Jack Russell very like Bounty but with only one brown eyepatch, and about three months younger. He was a 'rescue' dog, but is now much-loved, and the two of them have great games of tag. In fact an assortment of Jack Russells use the park—Daisy, smooth haired and from the same kennels as Bounty but about six months younger; Lucy, a broken coated, short legged little lady and Jack, similar in build to Lucy.

I mustn't forget the gentle, rough haired little dog that always likes to carry a stone in her mouth. She doesn't fraternise much, but trots along looking neither left nor right with a "My mission in life is to carry a stone" look. Then of course there is Heidi the Boxer, owned by my friends Maurice and Juliet (he too, writes). The two dogs have a rollicking chase-cum-wrestling match while we stand and chat, saving our legs.

One memorable day, Bounty was rooting around under his squirrel tree when he came across a canvas bag full of money. I met Maurice shortly after finding it and he offerred to take it to the Police for me as it was heavy. He had his car parked nearby and I was about a mile from home. The Police later reported that it was part of the proceeds from a £100,000 raid on the local Post Office the night before. ('Our' bag only contained copper coins and had obviously been jettisoned as too heavy or too much trouble to dispose of.)

All in all, Bounty, is an alert, friendly little dog and has no enemies, human or animal. Even most cats around here don't 'play the game' properly and stand their ground. In a house near me live the Embarrassing Cats - three of them who, when they meet Bounty, run purring to greet him. And the Ultimate Embarrassment is Isabella, a long haired black cat that GOES FOR A WALK off the lead with her owner and a little dog. "This," says Bounty, "is TOO MUCH!"

Chapter 11

Narrow Escapes

It is a good job Bounty is not a cat because he must have used up nine lives already. On the other hand, he may have a very busy Guardian Angel! Joan and I have been very good friends since our schooldays so it is not beyond the realms of possibility that Jamie, her much-loved and sadly departed little West Highland terrier could be keeping watch over MY pup from some doggy heaven. My reason for thinking this, is that for a few weeks after I had Bounty he took no notice of television, whatever the programme then suddenly one day jumped up and ran to the screen; there, trotting happily across a field was a little 'Jamie'. Had he recognised his 'mentor', I wonder?

After that, he became quite enthusiastic about animal programmes on the 'box'. Recently there was a series about cats and he sat bolt upright on my lap, gazing in fascination at the pictures, leaping down and running to the set when a particularly vicious-looking moggy appeared.

One day during the news a graph showing some business trend or other was depicted as a moving red line. He rushed to the TV as if to say, "Good Grief, the price of my shares is dropping!" (or else he thought it was a snake!) Sometimes he gazes in fascination at things he cannot possibly understand and I wonder what is going on in his little mind. He watched with interest while a family of forest gorillas squabbled and fought. An elephant lumbered across the screen - where did it go? Not behind the set, he's tried that! Giraffes undulated gracefully by and he's cocked his head from side to side with curiosity. What he makes of tanks, guns and man's inhumanity to man is anyone's guess.

Our ways must seem very strange to dogs. Do they question them, I wonder or just accept what we do? For instance, when I wake up, I take a small black object from under my pillow. It clicks - and suddenly there is a light which I shine at a small, rectangular object by my bed (a clock). Sometimes, after this performance I get up and prepare breakfast. Other times we snuggle down and go back to sleep, I lying on my side and Bounty 'sitting' on my lap. (At this moment he is fed up with me scratching away with a stick on a piece of paper and has just brought me Ring Thing (see chapter 16) for a game. I have hooked it over my toes and he is having a tug of war. At least my hands are free to go on writing). During the night I half-wake as the little body cuddles in closer. He is better than a hot water bottle, staying warm all night. (He has now put Ring Thing on his head to try and distract me and looks for all the world like an American Footballer!)

Another doggy puzzle must be the postmen who stick pieces of paper through the door and then go away without being admitted. No wonder dogs bark!

Books, too must seem strange. We open these objects and stare at them for hours on end, apparently immovable. Then there are cars - we get in, sit for a while and when we get out we are somewhere else. Not so Sharp. Cars mean VET and are to be avoided at all costs so he has never seen the sea. He wouldn't like it, anyway. He knows his place - a Working Farm Dog - and will not cross the boundaries of Jim's land. We have tried to persuade and cajole him but to no avail - he just lies down and refuses to budge saying, "You go on if you must, but I've a job to do, they can't run the farm without me," and we have to return by the same route to collect him, still on guard and waiting.

Anyhow, to get back to narrow escapes! Bounty has always loved squirrels. I felt it was safe for him to chase those - he hasn't a hope of catching them as they always take refuge out of reach - then came the time when one shot up a pine tree growing at an angle of some forty degrees after the October gales and suddenly, there he was, twenty feet up! I didn't know what to do - if I called he might fall, but I needn't have worried. Seeing the squirrel had transferred itself to another tree Bounty calmly turned and trotted down again with a "Curses, foiled again!" look as though he had been climbing trees all his life.

When he was still a pup we were at Corfe Castle in the garden of a pub which lay at the foot of the Purbeck hills. He was on his extending lead, when at the bottom of the garden he saw a rabbit. The garden was quiet and there were not many people there so I had placed the handle of the lead under the leg of the table, thinking this would give him room to sniff around and leave my hands free for my coffee. Suddenly he made a dash for the rabbit. With a whirring noise, the lead extended to its maximum length and the table leapt into the air, spilling my coffee all over the place. The tangled lead couldn't take the strain of the charging dog and snapped! Luckily the garden was enclosed and I caught him easily enough, but moments before we had crossed the busy main road to Swanage that passes through Corfe village!

Another time we had safely negotiated a road leading on to the moors when he saw a squirrel and was off before I could unclip him. This time the fastening on the extending lead (a different one) came undone. If it had been BEFORE we crossed the road the results didn't bear thinking about.

Once, leaving Branksome Recreation Ground he backed out of his new collar. It fitted him snugly when I bought it the week before (his other one having the 'D' ring break loose while he was pursuing a cat!) but he had since been swimming and the leather must have stretched. There he was, NAKED by the terribly busy road junction and traffic lights, while I held the lead and empty collar in my nerveless hands! I have NEVER moved so fast, gathering him into my arms and carrying him the two or three hundred yards home.

Then there was the time I passed his 'ordinary' lead through the loop of the handle and tied him to a post in Wareham while I went into Nellie Crumb's bakery for a loaf. I sometimes leave him outside my local library like this, checking him every couple of minutes, so he is used to it and sits quietly, watching everything that goes on with interest. This was very fortunate, as I hadn't tied the lead properly. There he sat, loose, by the side of the very busy main road! Joan goes pale when I tell her of our latest escapades.

One day, Bounty, Margaret and I were walking by the river Stour at Throop Mill. We had been there before, and then it had been lovely and peaceful - just the occasional dog-owner walking their dogs in the quiet of a summer evening, with ducks dabbling in the shallows and coots searching busily through the reeds for insects. THIS time there was something I had forgotten, though - the fishing season had started and the bank was dotted with fishermen and boys, accompanied by maggots, bait and the occasional fish.

"Great," thought Bounty, making a swoop (he is like a hoover) and a boy said woefully, "He's eaten my Spam - and it had a fish hook in it!" Oh horrors!

"VET - right away!" said Margaret positively.

"Well, the hook MIGHT have been in the small bit, and he's eaten the big bit," said the lad, looking alarmed.

"Now think carefully," I said, trying to keep calm, "This could be a matter of life or death!"

His chum said, "No, it's all right, he didn't eat the bit with the hook in it." Another life gone! (If I'd given him Spam he'd have turned up his nose).

When he was very small, Joan and I took him on Hambledon Hill. It was springtime and he had great fun, bounding over the turf of this massive Iron Age earthwork, looking for rabbits. The sides were quite steep and suddenly he slipped, rolling over and over down the side of the escarpment. "BOUNTY!" I screamed, visualising a broken neck or back, but he just shook himself and lolloped back up the hill again, looking slightly embarrassed.

Twice now, he has 'flown'. Joan and I were in a wood near Milton Abbas and Bounty had gone on ahead up a steep hill. "No, THIS way!" I called. He turned obediently and came galloping down the hill through the trees, faster and faster until his legs couldn't keep pace with his body, so he leapt - and flew the last few feet, landing safely, grinning up at us with tongue lolling and a "Wasn't that great?" look on his face. The next time was at Bramble Bay across the ferry from Sandbanks. You couldn't wish for a more beautiful place, with the Purbeck hills in the background and the islands of Poole Harbour sitting like clouds in a sea of pearl. A small cliff, about five feet high leads on to the beach. Bounty was ferreting about for rabbits but was out of sight. I called, and his jaunty little head appeared through the bracken. He ran to the cliff edge, saw it too late and sprang into space, landing in a bush! Undismayed, he picked himself out and came running towards me with, "Did you see that? Wasn't I clever!" written all over him.

"You WERE clever," I said, "But oh please, DO be more careful!" No wonder my hair is going grey!

Chapter 12
Encounters with Other Animals

Since owning a dog I have discovered that the usually reserved Englishman or woman becomes vociferous if they, too have a dog, pouring out their life story and that of their pet to complete strangers. Even children become chatty. On one such occasion we were walking near Hurn. A father and mother were ahead of us with their dog while their children tagged along with Margaret and me. We discovered how old they were, their ambitions for the future, the funny habits of their dog, where they lived and so on, and then they asked us questions in the same vein. The little girl (she was seven) had been quiet for a moment, pondering, then turned to me and said anxiously, "How old is your dog?"

"He is seven months," I told her.

She looked at me, considering, head on one side and said, "Do you think it was a good idea, you getting a puppy because ... well, you might not be able to look after it for much longer!" Obviously I looked as though I had one foot in the grave.

"Oh, don't worry," I assured her, "My friend Joan would look after him if anything happened to me!"

I recited this to Joan later and she laughed, saying the child at least had Bounty's welfare at heart, but also said she noticed how reticent people were now she no longer had a dog, so it would seem they bring out the best in people.

★ ★ ★

We were out in the wilds of Dorset one day, enjoying the beautiful scenery and fresh air when we came across about sixty young steers in a field alongside our footpath.

"Should we put him on the lead?" asked Joan.

"He should be all right. He doesn't chase the cows at the farm," I assured her. They were used to him and ignored his "Wuffs".

Now had the steer that stuck its head through the fence stood its ground, all would have been well but it was a timid young beast, obviously not used to dogs and took to its heels, charging off across the large field.

"Whoopee!" thought Bounty and ran at the wire 'lattice-type' sheep fence, attention fully on the steers. It was as well he hadn't reached full speed or he would have come out diced at the other side because he didn't see it, so intent was he on his prey.

"COME HERE!" I bellowed, making a grab but missing. Not he - he wriggled through and next minute the whole herd was stampeding! Joan and I looked at each other in dismay, then furtively around to see if anyone was watching the tiny white dog now in the far distance, having the whale of a time! Fortunately, nobody was in sight and eventually he came swaggering back, full of himself saying, "Did you see them go?"

It was no good telling him off, it was my fault entirely and I had learned my lesson, thanking Heaven they were fit young steers not in-calf heifers - it could have been disastrous. From them on, Bounty has always been on a lead in the presence of farm stock.

★ ★ ★

On a hot summer's day, Joan and I were walking in Delph Woods. Bounty didn't like the heat so we felt it would be more comfortable for him under the shade of the trees.

Suddenly she grabbed my arm. "What's that?" she hissed. There on the path in front of us in sinuous coils lay a black adder! Bounty had somehow passed it safely. Spotting us, it glided away into the undergrowth. Yelling at Bounty to follow we ran off in great haste in the opposite direction. I knew adders were rife on the sun-drenched hills of Purbeck and on the heathland but hadn't realised they lurked in woodland, too. Needless to say, we didn't go back to Delph Woods until the return of cooler weather.

★ ★ ★

As I've mentioned before, Bounty's favourite animals are squirrels. One day, we were passing our local pet shop when - oh joy! - in the window was a large cage with three scampering 'squirrels'. (Well, they were chipmunks really but he couldn't smell the difference through the plate glass). Standing on tiptoe on his hind legs he gazed at them in rapt admiration, absolutely fascinated. Around and around their cage they went, his little head following them like a spectator at Wimbledon. Then they paused, two inches from his nose, taunting him by nibbling at sunflower seeds held in their tiny paws and confident in their safety behind the glass. I had to drag him away and now, every time we go shopping in Parkstone we have to visit his 'squirrels'.

To his dismay, one day they weren't there! The pet shop lady saw us (we were well known by then) and said, "You are too early. We keep them in a room at the back overnight."

I dragged the unwilling Bounty to the newsagents and as we returned the pet shop lady was just putting the chipmunks in the window. The little white tail wagged joyously as up on his hind legs he went, gazing at his friends in delight.

At night, on our last walk of the day which takes us around the block he starts off at a gallop with his twenty-six foot extending lead at full length, towing me up the hill like a demented water-skier. This is a ritual and the one time he is allowed to 'pull'. Since the arrival of the chipmunks though, he began sitting at the kerb, looking back at me over his shoulder and then in the direction of Parkstone, indicating that he wanted to see his 'squirrels'. I explained that it was dark and they would be in bed so he reluctantly allowed me to continue our walk.

I have often watched dogs dreaming, paws and whiskers twitching but in addition he growls, wuffs, gives heartfelt sighs, wags his tail and one day frightened me to death by howling in his sleep! I had hoped the tail wagging was dreaming of greeting ME, but, thinking about it, I expect he had seen his 'squirrels'. I would love to know - they must be really vivid dreams!

Chapter 13

The First and Last Dog Show

Bounty was a really handsome little fellow by now. His coat had grown longer and people admired him when we stopped as he proudly but quite naturally adopted a show dog attitude, head and tail erect, rear legs back. When we resumed walking he soon forgot his poise and scampered ahead in a mad gallop, running free in the countryside. It was a joy and a pleasure to watch as he bounded and frisked like a lamb, pausing from time to time surreptitiously to make sure I was still behind him.

When he was six months old I took him back to the kennels at the breeder's request so he could see how he had turned out. He was delighted with him, insisting I entered him for a Show, saying I could make money the following year by putting him out to stud. That wasn't what I wanted for my little chum though. Maybe I was wrong, but I cannot for the life of me see how dogs can enjoy being cooped up in a small hutch for hours, often in hot weather, waiting their turn in the arena. Their owners insist the dogs love being shown but they are unable to roam in case they spoil their appearance. I was told of one that wasn't allowed in the sun as it might fade his coat; another was never let off the lead in case his muscles developed beyond the breed 'standard'. I realise Terrier Shows are not in the same category as Crufts but the Jack Russell Terrier Club of Great Britain standard states, 'Old scars or injuries, the result of work or accident should not be allowed to prejudice a terrier's chance in the show ring unless they interfere with its movement or with its utility for work or stud.' No, neither of those were for us.

When I was a child, I had a vision of obtaining an inner city deprived dog and letting him experience the pleasures of running free in the countryside, his true natural environment. Now I could let my own little dog enjoy these pleasures and it gave me a great sense of fulfilment.

However, at Dog Training one night (before Bounty was neutered) they announced the Club would be holding a Dog Show in aid of Riding for the Disabled and hoped everyone would give it their support, either by attending as spectators or entering their dogs.

I scanned the schedule and amongst the classes for 'Best Puppy', 'Obedience' and other impossible things was 'The Dog with the Most Appealing Eyes'! This was surely a 'cert'! Bounty's eyes are surrounded by a natural black 'eyeliner' making them appear even bigger and brighter than they are. I only have to say, "Squirrel!" and he cocks his head appealingly on one side - he couldn't lose!

The Show was set for a Sunday in September but the weather forecast was not good. Saturday produced heavy rain so I telephoned the Club to see what would happen if it were wet.

"Oh, we go ahead whatever the weather," I was told. "After all, there is no guarantee that a re-scheduled date would be any better."

"Right, we'll be there come hell or high water!" I answered with cheerful determination.

After a wet night, Sunday dawned soggily damp and misty. "Come on love," I called, "This is your big day!" He didn't need a bath as a couple of days previously he had been to Rockley on the shore of Poole harbour. He swam in the sea, fascinated as usual by the noisy jet-skis then swam again in the freshwater lake behind the shore, washing off the salt and sand, so he was lovely and white without further treatment.

At about 10.00am the rain stopped, which was great because the Show was due to start at noon and it would give the ground a chance to dry out a little. As insurance I put my wet weather gear in the car just in case, and we set off for Cowgrove.

We arrived at 11.30am, clutching our schedule - but where was everyone? It read 'Entries taken from 11.00am'. I checked it again, making sure we were at the correct venue. Yes, Wimborne Football Club grounds. A match had just finished on the nearby pitch so I asked a player if he knew where the Dog Show was being held.

"Dog Show? No idea!" he muttered disinterestedly, wiping mud-spatters from his cheek (his team must have lost!) and heading for the showers.

Then a lady arrived with a German Shepherd. We found a phone box and tried to telephone the Secretary but the line was engaged all the time. Other dog-owners began to arrive, one from as far away as London, another from Yeovil, until the car park was quite crowded. I still didn't recognise anyone in authority from the Dog Club and could see no notice anywhere saying the show had been cancelled. People were milling about uncertainly, then someone had the bright idea of asking at the Football Club bar.

"The Show's been rained off," they told us.

I was very annoyed. As it turned out, there wasn't another drop of rain all that afternoon and having been ASSURED it would go ahead regardless I felt we had wasted our day. I telephoned Margaret and Joe who had been coming to watch Bounty's debut but they had already left. I hung around until 12.30pm (Margaret had said they would be there at 12 o'clock) then made up my mind to go to Vi's at the farm. We were expected for tea, anyhow, so I invited myself to lunch as well. My sister never minds when we call, she is very good like that.

We drove along the lanes from Cowgrove to Lytchett and I glanced at the little fellow sitting contentedly in the front seat, wearing the seat belt Joan had brought him from Switzerland. "Why did I say I would enter you in a Show?" I asked him. "We don't need a judge to tell us you have beautiful eyes, we KNOW you have!" So when we got home later that evening I made him a rosette with, 'I'm a Winner' in the centre and he wore it proudly while I took his photo for posterity.

Standing in the kitchen that night making my Ovaltine, I watched the busy little figure preparing for bed, trotting between sitting room and bedroom with Big Bone, returning for a favourite stick (pine tastes best - the things I find on my bed in the morning!) and noticing a dog biscuit on the floor, tossed it into the air without a care in the world. I resolved then that THAT had been Bounty's First and Last Dog Show!

Chapter 14

The Stolen Car

It was around the time of Bounty's first birthday that his Guardian Angel was called into action yet again, this time in real earnest.
We parked at Sainsburys, intending to walk on the nearby moors before I left him in their car park to do my shopping. As I locked the car I heard police sirens nearby but took no notice, these being all too common in Alder Road, a main route of switchback hills between Branksome and Wallisdown.

We walked a short distance past a housing estate and across a green towards the heathland. As we crossed the green, Bounty stopped by a tree to do his business - and thank goodness he did - if we had been a few paces further on I dread to think what might have happened. Fishing a plastic bag from my pocket to 'do the necessary' I heard the police sirens coming nearer, then with a scream of tyres a white car with a smashed off-side came hurtling around the corner towards us. I grabbed Bounty in my arms, pressing myself against a hedge. The car drove along a footpath between houses and garages, narrowly missing an electricity pylon and vanished on to the heath. Suddenly a Police Dog Handler van appeared in hot pursuit, attempted to turn and hit the wooden bollards surrounding the green. The van actually flew in the air then shot downhill where we had just been walking, through more bollards on the other side of the green and smashing into a parked car! The police dog was barking furiously from the van then the handler opened the door and got out, shaken but unhurt. The drama wasn't over yet - with a cacophony of sirens two more police cars appeared and screeched to a halt alongside the wrecked van.

Still clutching a trembling Bounty to my chest I yelled, "OVER THERE!" indicating the moors. The police cars accelerated in reverse with more screeching of tyres, turned in the direction I had

The Stolen Car

shown them, drove around the corner and surrounded the white car where it had come to a halt on the moors.

I felt shaken and sick with shock. Putting Bounty down again we walked a little way around the corner and there he WAS sick, poor little soul.

I was wary of going on the heath, not knowing if anyone was at large and fearing we may be held hostage at knifepoint or something equally dramatic, so we walked around the block instead. Morbid curiosity drew me back to the scene where the road was being chalk-marked by the police.

"Is it safe to go on the moors, please?" I asked.

"Yes, love," replied a handsome bearded policeman. "It was a stolen car and we've got the driver. He rammed another car up the road as well. I'm sorry we've put you to this inconvenience!" Who said our policemen are not wonderful?

"Not at all," I replied warmly, "I'm only too relieved you caught the blighter!"

We continued our walk on the moors, but little Bounty wasn't such a happy dog that day. Indeed, the next time we went there a week later, he kept glancing nervously towards the scene of the incident. To this day, if he hears a police siren his tail drops and the little face looks anxiously up at me for reassurance. Thankfully though, he has adjusted to the moors now and romps once more in the stream and once again chases the squirrels into the oaks and silver birches.

Chapter 15

Worrying Times

Something wasn't right. Bounty hadn't eaten his dinner and didn't look at all happy. At 8.30pm he asked to go to bed which was unusual, so I did too, thinking, "Ah well, I can read for a couple of hours." I made myself comfortable, while keeping an anxious eye on Bounty who was lying against my legs. After a few minutes he raised his head, then stood rather uncertainly, creeping up the bed into the circle of my arms for solace and comfort and curled up against my body. As he inhaled his body trembled and I could hear his tummy gurgling. We stayed like that until the early hours, I cat-napping from time to time while he drifted off to sleep. Every time I woke I listened to his breathing until gradually I noticed it becoming more normal. At around 5.00am he woke, jumped off the bed and went out of the room. Climbing from my bed to see if he wanted to go out, I heard the 'ting ting' of his name tag against his bowl - Bounty was eating his dinner! Oh, the relief!

A couple of days later I had an appointment with my hairdresser. I was changing to a short, easy to manage hairstyle which would cope with being out of doors in all weathers - so the coming of Bounty had even changed my appearance! Joan said she would have him for the morning and then we could go for a walk in the afternoon. She lives at Oakdale, some three miles from me and my hairdresser is quite close to home. I always wear the same jumper when having my hair cut as, no matter how careful they are, little ends of hair seem to stick around the neck acting like a hair shirt. I told Joan I would call home on the way to change my jumper, and that I would see her about 12 o'clock.

I opened my front door - no little dog to greet me and everything so quiet! Had I really lived like this for five and a half years? Then I saw on the carpet a single yellow dog-biscuit with no-one there to eat it. It looked so lonely! A lump came to my throat, I missed him so! "You silly old fool!" I told myself, "you will see him in ten minutes!"

★ ★ ★

It was a week later and again Bounty couldn't seem to settle, shifting from place to place during the afternoon then going out into the hall. That in itself was unusual as he always likes to keep an eye on me and not be on his own, so after a few minutes I went to look for him. He was standing on the rug looking most unhappy, his usually alert ears drooping.

"What is it, love?" I asked, but he just stood there looking dejected. He hadn't eaten or drunk anything again all day but when I picked him up I heard his tummy gurgling and rumbling loudly. Although I was half-way through my tea I rang the Vet right away to get Bounty examined while he still showed the symptoms. They were able to fit me in if I went there and then so within ten minutes we were in the waiting room, tea abandoned.

Bounty suddenly recalled his last visit and shook uncontrollably. "It's all right, love," I promised, "The Vet will make you BETTER."

"It's not very nice for us," the young receptionist said, "We're animal lovers too but they hate coming to see us."

I explained to the Vet what was wrong and that the same thing had happened the previous week as well.

"His temperature is very slightly raised," he said, "and he has a tummy upset. An injection and pills will soon put him right." So it was nothing serious, thank Heavens!

I explained that I found it difficult giving him pills as his jaws are so strong and my fingers are somewhat arthritic.

"You MUST persist," he said firmly. "If in years to come he has a heart condition he may have to take pills every day. Still, with THESE you can grind them to powder and sprinkle them on his food if you like."

I mentioned that Bounty had been scratching his ear the night before, and wondered if an infection he'd had a few months earlier had returned, as he had curled his lip at me when I examined it.

"You MUST stop him doing that. Show him you are the boss!" he told me.

"But how else can he let me know he is in pain?" I asked reasonably. "He wasn't trying to bite me." I wanted to explain that living on a one-to-one basis with a dog and being in each other's company for most of the 24 hours in each day we had an understanding rather than me being the 'boss'. The Vet was busy though, and as he assured me the ear wasn't infected I let matters rest.

Bounty is fine again now, thank goodness, playing games, chasing squirrels and lying back in ecstasy while I tickle his tum. I suppose these things are sent to try us - and they do!

Chapter 16

Bounty's First Birthday

The fourth of October was ringed on my calendar as a day of importance - my pup was one year old. The postman came at 6.45am and Bounty hurled himself furiously at the letter box as usual. He is an excellent watchdog. To quote Dr. Desmond Morris, "A barking dog doesn't mean 'let's kill the postman'. It means 'something here needs watching and I might need you as back up.'"

"It's all right, they're for you!" I told him, picking up the letters and giving him a cuddle. There were four cards, from Vi, Joan and daughter Jill, and of course myself although I admit to quietly sliding mine in with the others to save the stamp.

I read the cards out to him. Joan's of course was very clever. She always refers to herself as 'Auntie Joan' to Bounty. Her card read, "From a special Auntie" (she had amended it from "To a ...") and there was a picture of two women in walking gear with sticks which we use in the country when the going is slippery. One woman had brown hair (Joan) and one grey (me, although she is three months older than I am, dammit!) and behind them ran a little brown and white dog carrying their knapsack!

"Oh look," I told him, "It's from Auntie Joan," and let him have a sniff to identify her. Then producing a large cardboard box, I put it on the bed saying, "There you are love, Happy Birthday!" His head was already poking around, trying to find an opening, tail wagging frantically as he lifted out an enormous cooked bone. "WOW!" his face said. I also gave him a waterproof coat and his very own box of tissues, so the bungalow soon resembled a snow storm.

After a quick breakfast, I said "Come on then, Birthday Boy - walkies!" He raced out to the car, settling himself in his seat. It was a beautiful early October day. Leaves were taking on their autumn tints and the mists of early morning had cleared leaving bejewelled cobwebs on hedges and bushes. I decided we would go to his favourite rabbity place, East Hill Corfe Castle. There were no animals grazing in the field crossed by the path so I let him off the lead and he was soon poking around in the brambles and gorse. He only spotted one rabbit but the scents were present so he was quite content. In sheltered places wild flowers still bloomed - corn cockle, yellow cinquefoil and the grey seeds of old man's beard.

Later, in Corfe village we kept meeting classes of schoolchildren from the Baden Powell and St. Peter School to whom I had given a talk about Corfe Castle the previous week.

"Look, there's the writer lady!" said one of the first group.

"Hello Miss Wilnecker," said some of the others politely, smiling in recognition. This was repeated throughout the village. Well, there were five groups of thirty children and Corfe is a very small village! I introduced Bounty to some of them, as I had mentioned him in my talk (naturally!) explaining that it was his birthday.

"Hold it there, Miss!" said one youngster and took our photo. Bounty swaggered back to the car with a truly nonchalant expression, taking fame in his stride. Before we left, we called at the National Trust shop where he is well known and had a special birthday fuss made of him before making our way home. After all, I had to prepare his birthday tea and Joan, John and Jill were coming.

At about 6.30pm the doorbell rang and Bounty dashed importantly to see who it was.

"Happy Birthday!" chorused Joan and Jill, while John looked a little embarrassed by these daft women.

"Pressies first!" said Joan, when I had taken their coats. Jill produced a pack of Bounty's favourite Beef Smackos and he politely ate one there and then to show his appreciation.

Joan and John had a beautifully wrapped box which I helped Bounty open. We discovered a lovely toy which I can only call a 'Ring Thing'. It resembles three bananas joined at the top and bottom and is made of red rubber. It can be thrown, tugged or bounced and is easy for doggie mouths to pick up. He especially likes being swung off the ground in circles, holding on only by his teeth like a frantic trapeze artist. It looks fearsome but when I stop (exhausted!) he pushes the

Ring Thing at me again, tail wagging hopefully, saying, "More, more!"

We all sat down for tea (chicken salad with Bounty's own bowl of roast chicken along with us in the dining room - well, it was HIS party!) Then came the birthday cake, meringue gateau with a single candle on top. Bounty had a piece of course, as he loves creamy things as a very occasional special treat, but always cleans his teeth afterwards with a hard dog biscuit.

When tea was finished, I asked Bounty to show his guests the other presents.

"Where's your Big Bone?" I asked, and he rooted around in his toy box (where he had hidden it) which always stands in the corner of the sitting room until he found it. It was a heavy weight for a little Jack Russell but with great determination, tugging and heaving it finally clonked on the floor and he looked up at Joan triumphantly.

"Clever boy!" we cried in unison and he sat there, looking pleased with himself.

★ ★ ★

Another month has passed and we have just returned from a walk on the moors. The heath was tawny-gold in its autumn colours with the damp branches of willows near the stream showing darkly against the afternoon sky. A kestrel quartered the hilltop undisturbed by our passing, then a man walking five assorted dogs approached. Bounty, outnumbered, made himself scarce - he is only a very small dog - returning as soon as they had passed. You could see him thinking, "Scared? ME! Never - just being careful!" Rain had been forecast so he wore his little raincoat and snuffled around in the bushes after an interesting scent. Suddenly he emerged with the Velcro fastening across his chest undone, jacket folded neatly back from the belt around his middle displaying the plaid lining, looking for all the world like a trendy young teenager.

Nowadays when I see people walking without dogs it seems as though there is something missing - they appear incomplete - yet that was me not so long ago.

So here we are; in my ignorance I have made many mistakes, but in spite of them Bounty and I are great friends and companions and he has more than compensated for my errors by his good manners. When I began, I said I had good friends and relations - but they, of course have their own families which are naturally closer to them than I am. With the best will in the world I am not their first priority but with my little Bounty we are both the most important things in each other's lives - our personal Number One.

I have discovered that Jack Russells are alert, playful, affectionate, intelligent, fun-loving, inquisitive, mischievous and sometimes independent - but not when they need you!

Next week, we will have been together for exactly one year. The months fly by so quickly, but please God there will be many, many more years together. Little did I realise how much he would change my life - my dress, habits, outlook on life, my home - even as I finish hoovering it seems my once immaculate bungalow has white dog hairs everywhere and dog biscuits crunch underfoot in the goatskin rug. There is a large bone hidden under the bed and his prized possessions litter the sitting room. But there is one thing of which I am certain - I wouldn't change anything now - not for the world!

BOUNTY—*the tale of a dog*

"Oh—you've bought a guinea pig!" said Vi.

"Is this my new home?"

BOUNTY—*the tale of a dog*

He enjoyed Joan's Christmas party.

BOUNTY—the tale of a dog

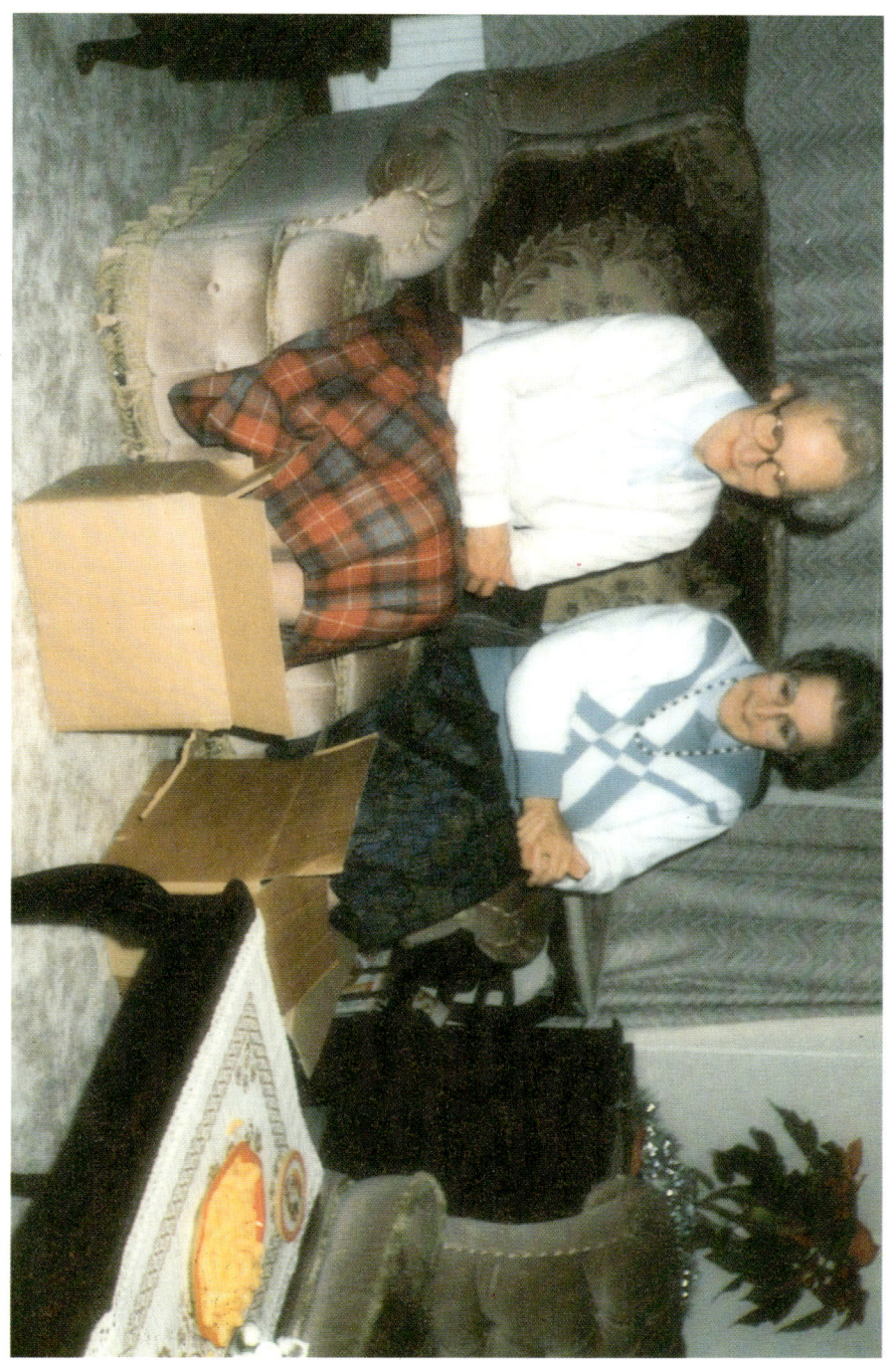

The guests protected their ankles with cardboard boxes.

BOUNTY—the tale of a dog

Modelling his sheepskin coat.

He wasn't often destructive—but when he was, it was spectacular!

BOUNTY—the tale of a dog

There goes the bathroom mat again!

BOUNTY—*the tale of a dog*

"Got to help her with the washing".

BOUNTY—*the tale of a dog*

"Who needs a Labrador?"

He naturally adopts a show dog stance.

BOUNTY—the tale of a dog

"I help in the garden, too!"

BOUNTY—*the tale of a dog*

BOUNTY—the tale of a dog

"I've found the car keys—now try and get them!"

BOUNTY—*the tale of a dog*

The tortoises came to stay for a week.

BOUNTY—*the tale of a dog*

"Where did that OTHER squirrel go?"

BOUNTY—*the tale of a dog*

The author holding Bounty, with Joan at Studland.

BOUNTY—the tale of a dog

Bounty and the Beast in woods near Badbury Rings.

BOUNTY—*the tale of a dog*

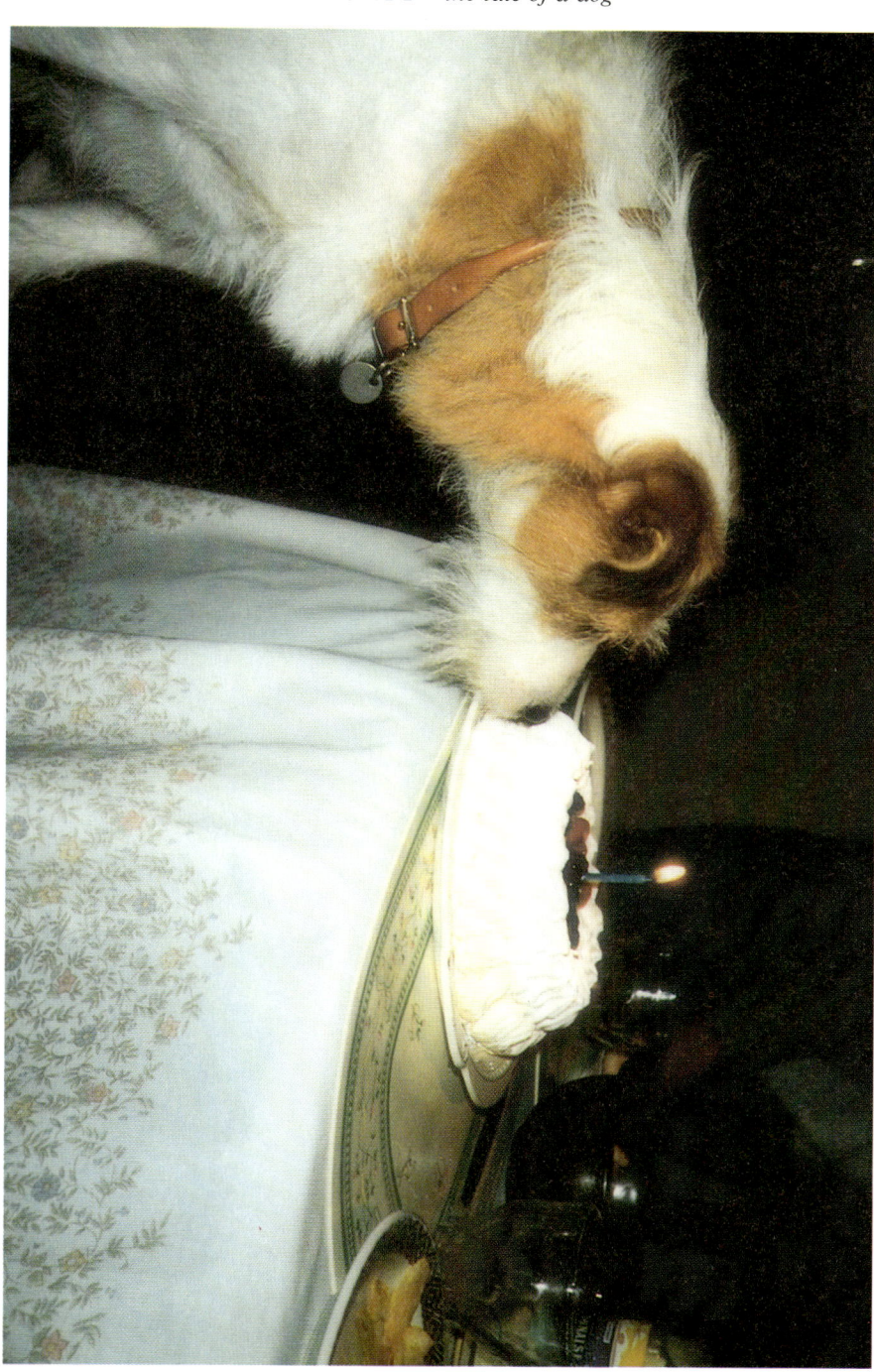

His first Birthday Cake.

BOUNTY—the tale of a dog

"It's SUCH a hard life—being a dog!"